PRINCIPLES

FOR

ENLARGEMENT

Mastering the Principles of Personal and Financial Growth

MARCELLINUS

C.U

This publication aims to offer general information on the covered subject matter. However, laws and practices can vary between states and are subject to change. As each factual situation is unique, specific advice should be tailored to individual circumstances. Therefore, readers are advised to consult with their own advisors regarding their particular situations.

The author has taken reasonable precautions in preparing this book and believes the facts presented are accurate as of the writing date. Nevertheless, neither the author nor the publisher assumes any responsibility for errors or omissions. The author and publisher explicitly disclaim any liability arising from the use or application of the information in this book, and it is not intended to serve as legal, financial, or other professional advice for individual situations.

Published by:
BelieversWatch

This book, PRINCIPLES FOR ENLARGEMENT, is dedicated to those navigating life's crossroads, grappling with the impact of the current economic crisis, and feeling a sense of helplessness regarding their financial future. Despite the challenges, I want to convey that now is the opportune moment for you to seize control of your destiny. Devoting my life to teaching and uplifting others within the kingdom, I am confident that this book will equip you with the knowledge necessary to construct and sustain your wealth for the years ahead. By grasping the true essence of how enlargement operates, you'll be empowered to embark on the journey of building the life you aspire to achieve.

Table of Contents

CHAPTER ONE

THE PRIOTITY OF PERSONAL AND FINANCIAL GROWTH

PRINCIPLES FOR ENLARGEMENT

The Bible in Isaiah 54:2 urges us to enlarge the place of our tent and stretch forth the curtains of our habitation. Enlargement, therefore, becomes our responsibility. While God is eager to propel us into expansive territories, there are essential steps we must take to experience enlargement on every side.

The significance of enlargement lies in the fact that certain responsibilities and blessings cannot be entrusted to us until we expand our capacity. Our actions are intricately linked to our capacity, and even though God loves us, there are numerous things He cannot commit to us unless we are enlarged.

In the kingdom, commitment is not solely based on love but on maturity. Just as you wouldn't entrust a car to a child, God doesn't entrust certain responsibilities to us until we have matured in capacity. It's not a matter of God's love; it's a matter of our ability to handle the entrusted tasks.

While witnessing others excel in their service to God, some may question why their situation seems different, wondering if God loves them enough. The truth is, it's not about love; it's about capacity. Can you handle the responsibilities if they are committed to you?

PRINCIPLES FOR ENLARGEMENT

In the same way, a parent wouldn't let a child drive, God won't entrust significant tasks to us until we've matured spiritually. The objective of this book is to emphasize God's desire to bring individuals to a place of capacity where greater commitments can be entrusted to them.

Enlargement, as discussed in this book, aims to elevate you to a higher pedestal in the Spirit, preparing you to handle greater commitments. I am confident that as you journey through these pages, you will ascend to greater heights in your relationship with God, ready to embrace more significant responsibilities and experiences in His service. In Jesus' precious name, Amen.

CHAPTER TWO

THE
PRINCIPLE OF
GROWTH

PRINCIPLES FOR ENLARGEMENT

The first principle for achieving enlargement is encapsulated in The Principle of Growth, as expounded in Galatians 4:1 – "The heir, as long as he is a child, does not differ at all from a servant, though he is master of all." This scripture underscores three crucial insights:

Firstly, the child is unquestionably the heir, yet the critical query is whether they are prepared to handle the responsibility. Despite being the rightful owner, the child is often perceived and treated as a servant until they mature.

Secondly, an heir can unwittingly be relegated to the status of a servant if maturity is lacking. In the kingdom, what you receive is contingent upon your level of maturity. If you aspire for enlargement, mastering the principles of growth becomes imperative because the extent to which you can occupy is intricately tied to your growth in the kingdom.

Enlargement, therefore, hinges on your ability to choose between operating as an heir or as a servant. To step into occupying greater territories, you must willingly pay the price of growth. Growth is not a spontaneous occurrence; it requires deliberate actions. Similar to physical growth, spiritual growth demands nourishment – through the consumption of the Word, exercise, and periods of rest.

PRINCIPLES FOR ENLARGEMENT

Regrettably, some individuals in the kingdom seek prophecies without shouldering the responsibility to grow. Prophecies, instead of becoming empowering, can overwhelm those unprepared for the responsibilities they entail. The power to manifest these prophecies is only unleashed through personal growth.

To truly be enlarged, the scriptures must transform into your life's philosophy. Many believers draw wisdom from worldly adages and proverbs, functioning in the kingdom of light with the philosophy of another realm. This incongruity impedes their ability to receive the power and blessings of the kingdom they inhabit.

Whether desiring a successful marriage, financial breakthrough, or anointing, true enlargement is contingent upon your commitment to grow in these areas. The responsibility to grow necessitates an unwavering dedication to studying the Word and engaging in prayer.

The first principle of enlargement, The Principle of Growth, unequivocally asserts that your growth is intricately tied to the Word and Prayer (Joshua 1:8). As the Word takes root in your life, your capacity expands, and your environment responds. Your surroundings react not to your appearance but to the substance you carry. Therefore, to experience true enlargement, elevate the quality of what you carry (Proverbs 4:20-23).

Enlargement becomes evident when the Word saturates your spirit, influencing every aspect of your life. It goes beyond head knowledge to a profound internalization that transforms your environment. To be enlarged, cultivate the grace to consume the Word daily, for as Jesus emphasized, "Man shall not live by bread alone but by every word that proceeds from the mouth of God."

The Principle of Growth emphasizes that your commitment to daily intake of the Word and fervent prayer is pivotal for true enlargement. The Word creates a spiritual environment where your capacity is enlarged, setting the stage for genuine growth and transformation.

CHAPTER THREE

THE
PRINCIPLE OF
WARFARE

PRINCIPLES FOR ENLARGEMENT

Taking over demands relentless effort; even the ground you currently hold can slip away if you ease up. Yet, many remain complacent, believing that destiny will unfold at its own pace. Ask yourself, how many years have passed? Why hasn't it happened yet? Beware of deception; nothing here happens by chance—it's all intentional, and if you don't make it happen, it won't.

To avoid mediocrity, rouse yourself and engage in the battle. This kingdom favors only those who fight. As Matthew 11:12 states, "And from the days of John the Baptist until now the kingdom of heaven suffers violence, and the violent take it by force." In this realm, you don't choose warfare; warfare chooses you. Therefore, be prepared at all times. Fainting in times of trouble indicates insufficient strength.

The Bible warns, "...the devil is prowling like a roaring lion looking for whom he might devour" (1 Peter 5:8). You don't instigate the fight; it comes looking for you. Stay battle-ready; otherwise, enlargement will remain elusive. Throughout the Old Testament, conquests were achieved through battles. Joshua conquered 31 nations through relentless warfare. Nothing is given in this kingdom; even your inheritance must be seized.

Consider Deuteronomy 2:24 – "Rise, take your journey, and cross over the River Arnon. Look, I have given into your hand Sihon the

PRINCIPLES FOR ENLARGEMENT

Amorite..." God has given it to you, yet you must contend for it. God acknowledges that nothing is given; everything is taken. Therefore, those seeking enlargement must aggressively pursue their destinies.

Your promotion won't come as you sit idly, and blessings won't befall you while you sleep. Enlargement is captured in the arena of warfare. A believer unwilling to fight will not experience growth, for this kingdom is inherently opposed to you.

Christians are endangered in this world, facing tribulations for standing in truth. Overcoming requires active fighting; silence and passivity lead to subjugation. Every impactful person is a fighter. Spare time isn't leisure time—it's warfare time. Sitting for hours watching movies is not leisure; it's neglecting your battleground. Those conquering territories utilize their free time wisely.

The principle is clear: fight to conquer. The battle is relentless, but those embracing it rise to conquer new territories. The Bible urges believers to rise and take up their journey; failing to rise leads to perishing (Isaiah 60:1). Light may have come, but it only shines upon those who stand. Battle is required for standing; hence, "having done all to stand, stand therefore" (Ephesians 6:13). Enlargement is not a gift; it's achieved through battles fought by warriors.

PRINCIPLES FOR ENLARGEMENT

Today, less than 2% rule the world while over 98% are either servants or slaves. Civilization may term them "civilized servants," but audacity drives those who rule. If you desire enlargement, find your battlefield, fight, and conquer.

Principles for Enlargement - Warfare:

- Diligence
- Discipline
- Focus
- Hard Work

The second principle emphasizes that possession follows conquest. Without conquering, there is no ownership; without fighting, there is no victory. The notion of possessing without conquering is self-deception; time will reveal a wasted lifetime. In this kingdom, you don't ask for warfare; it seeks you out.

CHAPTER FOUR

THE PRINCIPLE OF VISION

PRINCIPLES FOR ENLARGEMENT

The Third Principle for Enlargement is The Principle of Vision. It asserts that you can only possess what you envision, making the devil's agenda to blind people all the more strategic. Visionary blindness isn't about physical sight but the inability of the mind to perceive. To attain enlargement, one must develop the ability to see, as it is what is visualized that ultimately becomes reality (Genesis 13:14-15).

Abraham, chosen for blessings by God, was instructed to leave his father's house and kindred to a land God would show him. God emphasized the importance of seeing to possess, declaring blessings upon him. However, upon arriving in the promised land, Abraham couldn't see anything and wandered until God revealed the principles. Sight, in this context, goes beyond the physical; it requires a spiritual insight into God's promises.

The devil's tactic is to blind hearts through carnality (2 Corinthians 4:3). Sensuality leads to spiritual blindness, hindering creative thinking and innovation. A generation consumed by lust and seduction loses its mental power. Notably, other cultures focus on developing intellectual prowess, exemplified by the Arabian prince's observation about China's educational priorities.

PRINCIPLES FOR ENLARGEMENT

To counteract this, the vent for vision in the kingdom is the Word, representing light. The Bible advises against opening one's spirit to nonsensical influences. The scriptures, written for our learning, provide patience and comfort, inspiring hope (Romans 15:4 KJV). Immersing oneself in God's Word opens the spirit and facilitates enlargement.

Enlargement involves seeing beyond current limitations. Walking with God expands one's perspective, allowing for plans and budgets that transcend national boundaries. The principle of vision asserts that what you see is what you can possess, and God's actions are limited by the scope of your vision (Ephesians 3:20). Your mental faculties, including imagination and creativity, play a vital role. If you cannot visualize it, God will not exceed those limits, emphasizing the correlation between your vision and manifestation.

The third principle of enlargement, the Principle of Vision, underscores the significance of seeing in the spiritual sense. It highlights the importance of developing a vision aligned with God's promises to overcome limitations and experience true enlargement.

CHAPTER FIVE

THE
PRINCIPLE OF
FAITHFULNESS

PRINCIPLES FOR ENLARGEMENT

The Fourth Principle of enlargement is the Principle of Faithfulness. It asserts that to achieve growth, one must first prove faithful in small matters. The pathway to greatness is reserved for those who demonstrate faithfulness with modest responsibilities; indeed, big opportunities are not bestowed upon those unfaithful in the small tasks (Luke 16:10).

The measurement of faithfulness occurs through service. Enlargement in any area demands a willingness to serve first, proving one's faithfulness before the omniscient God. In a generation characterized by rebellion, where service may be perceived as a waste of time, the principle emphasizes the importance of apprenticeship. How can one be a master without first being an apprentice, and how can one be a trusted master without earning trust as an apprentice?

The track record of service is crucial when seeking what one desires. God's trust is earned through a heart dedicated to service (Jeremiah 17:10). Faithfulness extends beyond the act of serving; it encompasses a commitment to both the current responsibilities and the envisioned future. This commitment fuels determination, persistence, and a refusal to accept defeat, paving the way for larger opportunities.

PRINCIPLES FOR ENLARGEMENT

The principle emphasizes that faithfulness in small matters is a precursor to faithfulness in more significant responsibilities. The biblical principle states that if one cannot be faithful with little, more will not be entrusted to them. Even the little that one possesses may be taken away if unfaithfulness persists (Matthew 13:12). The cycle perpetuates as the rich, who seek more challenges and opportunities, receive additional resources, while the poor, often consumed by complaints, may lose even what little they possess.

To pursue expansion and enlargement, one must remain faithful to the responsibilities currently entrusted. Faithfulness becomes the bedrock upon which enlargement is built. The judgment is based on what is in one's hand, emphasizing the significance of proving oneself with existing responsibilities before aspiring to greater ones. In summary, the Principle of Faithfulness underlines the essential role of faithful service in achieving enlargement and taking on more significant responsibilities.

CHAPTER SIX

THE PRINCIPLE OF THE BLESSINGS

PRINCIPLES FOR ENLARGEMENT

The Fifth Principle of enlargement is known as The Blessings – highlighting that enlargement is intricately tied to the power of blessings. To experience significant growth, one must receive spoken words of blessing. Throughout history, those who achieved supernatural enlargement were recipients of divine blessings. Abraham, Isaac, and Jacob, for instance, experienced explosive growth as a result of divine blessings spoken over them.

The catalyst for explosive growth in an individual's life often lies in the blessings and prophetic words spoken over them. While diligence, focus, and hard work contribute to success, the supernatural element of blessings plays a crucial role. Recognizing and honoring those who carry blessings becomes essential, including parents and spiritual mentors chosen by the Lord to guide one's life.

The principle emphasizes the importance of discernment and honor towards carriers of blessings, such as parents and spiritual leaders. Failure to honor and respect these figures may hinder one's path to enlargement. The principle draws attention to a prevalent issue where individuals, despite hard work and skills, struggle to progress due to the absence of blessings. In such cases, people may work tirelessly yet experience limited success, lacking the essential blessings that fuel enlargement.

Honoring parents is highlighted as a crucial aspect, with the reminder that it is the first law accompanied by a promise (Ephesians 6:2). Acknowledging the pain caused to parents and respecting their position becomes a key factor in the journey toward enlargement.

The principle discourages the harmful practice of comparing oneself to others and emphasizes the importance of understanding the unique blessings each individual carries. In a spiritual world, blessings play a pivotal role in determining the course of one's life. The principle concludes with a reflection on the mysteries of blessings, suggesting that those who lack this crucial element may find themselves laboring tirelessly yet experiencing weariness and limited success.

In essence, The Blessings principle underscores the transformative power of spoken words of blessing in achieving enlargement, emphasizing the need to honor and recognize carriers of blessings in one's life.

CHAPTER SEVEN

THE
PRINCIPLE OF
GIFT

PRINCIPLES FOR ENLARGEMENT

The Sixth Principle of enlargement centers around your Gift – Proverbs 18:16 states that "a man's gift makes room for him." When you begin to master and refine your unique talents, this gift becomes a source of enlargement, applicable both within and outside the kingdom, embodying universal principles.

In addition to your formal training, it is essential to identify, develop, and master your gift. This singular ability sets you apart.

Consider the case of Lionel Messi, who, upon winning his 6th Ballon d'Or, received a $150,000 Rolex watch from a company seeking his endorsement. The impact was profound – as Messi wore the watch, orders flooded in, enough to sustain the company for a decade. This illustrates how a gift, when expertly wielded, can elevate an individual to a god-like status.

During the last World Cup (Qatar 2022), nations prayed for Messi's success due to his mastery and humble expression of his gift. His proficiency earned him the goodwill of leaders and the entire world.

Your gift has the potential to provide you with more than ten lifetimes of training. If true enlargement is your goal, discover your gift, refine it, and become its master. When you reach a level where no one

PRINCIPLES FOR ENLARGEMENT

else can use your gift as uniquely as you do, kings, nations, and your generation will celebrate you.

It is crucial to recognize that people relate to you not just because they love you but because of the value your gift brings. If someone neglects their gift and seeks favor forcefully, they may attract reproach.

An intriguing example is the suspension of marriage laws in Saudi Arabia for Cristiano Ronaldo. This act, in a nation known for strict adherence to laws and values, underscores the powerful influence of a person's gift.

For believers, God has endowed three major gifts: righteousness, eternal life, and the Holy Spirit. Struggles often stem from neglecting or failing to develop these gifts. When you invest time in building your gift, you will be astonished by the magnitude of enlargement and expansion it brings.

Consider the case of Barack Obama, whose gift of eloquence and compelling speech propelled him to the presidency. His ability to articulate ideas without a script for an hour, like a flowing river, showcases the impact of mastering one's gift.

PRINCIPLES FOR ENLARGEMENT

The overwhelming influence of gifting even affects one's enemies. Therefore, anyone sincerely seeking enlargement must take responsibility for discovering, developing, and refining their gift.

CHAPTER EIGHT

THE PRINCIPLE OF GIVING AND SACRIFICE

PRINCIPLES FOR ENLARGEMENT

Utilizing the resources God bestows upon us is integral to achieving enlargement, and there are three fundamental approaches to managing these resources.

The first method involves saving resources. While saving is a commendable practice, it represents the most basic way to handle one's resources.

A more advanced strategy is investment. Those who invest are considered superior to mere savers. Wealthy individuals recognize the power of investment and engage in it to multiply their resources significantly. Consequently, when seeking enlargement, affluent individuals often prioritize investments.

However, there exists a realm superior to investment,, and it is referred to as **SACRIFICE**. In addition to investment, integrating sacrifice into one's financial approach holds a unique significance.

When God aimed to enlarge Abraham, He emphasized the importance of sacrifice. Despite being a businessman, God conveyed to Abraham that merely investing was insufficient.

PRINCIPLES FOR ENLARGEMENT

In Genesis 22:1, Abraham's act of sacrifice paved the way for divine blessings. Remarkably, some of the world's wealthiest billionaires are renowned for their extravagant philanthropy. Giving is not confined to religious doctrine; it is a universal law for achieving enlargement. This principle was demonstrated by Noah when he offered sacrifices to God.

Prominent figures such as Warren Buffett exemplify this concept. Buffett has publicly declared that he won't burden his children with the weight of his wealth. Instead, he advocates for building intelligence to create wealth. Moreover, he plans to donate 80% of his wealth to charitable causes upon retirement.

These wealthy individuals consistently contribute substantial amounts, often millions of dollars, toward poverty alleviation and health improvement. In stark contrast, some individuals with limited resources may resist giving even when assistance is offered. The generous nature of the affluent is evident when they proactively identify and support needs within their communities.

The principle underscores that people often give their way into greatness. Sacrifices made today can effectively secure a prosperous future. The laws of nature and God recognize and respect this

PRINCIPLES FOR ENLARGEMENT

commitment to giving. Therefore, adopting a lifestyle of giving, guided by personal conviction and maturity, can pave the way for enlargement. It is this maturity that positions individuals to carry the burdens of nations and contribute significantly to the betterment of society.

CONCLUSION

A
JOURNEY TOWARD
UNPRECEDENTED
GROWTH

PRINCIPLES FOR ENLARGEMENT

As we draw the curtains on "Mastering the Principles of Personal and Financial Growth," we find ourselves at the crossroads of enlightenment and transformation. The principles unveiled within these pages transcend the boundaries of mere financial success; they are the keys to unlocking a life of unparalleled enlargement in every facet.

In the pages, we navigated the landscape of diligence, recognizing it as the cornerstone upon which personal and financial empires are built. We encountered the inevitability of warfare, understanding that battles are not hindrances but gateways to progress. The principle of vision urged us to rise above visionary blindness, teaching us that what we see, we can possess.

Faithfulness emerged as a faithful companion on the journey, reminding us that small tasks pave the way for grand responsibilities. We reveled in the blessings that shower upon the faithful and those who honor them, understanding that they are not merely divine favors but powerful agents of enlargement.

Our exploration extended to the discovery and refinement of our unique gifts, understanding that these gifts, once mastered, become the catalysts for personal and financial elevation. And in the spirit of giving and

PRINCIPLES FOR ENLARGEMENT

sacrifice, we unearthed the universal law that generosity is the gateway to greatness, both personally and financially.

As we reflect on these principles, remember that their integration into your life is not a one-time event but a continuous journey. The book serves as a guide, a compass pointing you in the direction of extraordinary growth. It is not just a compilation of principles; it is an invitation to embark on a lifelong expedition of self-discovery and prosperity.

In the events of your life, weave these principles into the very fabric of your being. Apply them diligently, fight your battles with wisdom, embrace a clear and expansive vision, be faithful in every endeavor, cherish and value the blessings that come your way, cultivate and deploy your unique gifts, and let the spirit of generosity and sacrifice flow through your actions.

Remember, the journey to enlargement is not about the destination; it's about the person you become along the way. The principles outlined here are not constraints but liberators, providing the framework for a life marked by significance, impact, and unprecedented growth.

As you step into the realm of mastering these principles, may your personal and financial horizons stretch beyond the ordinary, reaching the extraordinary. May you become a living testament to the transformative power of these principles, a beacon inspiring others to embark on their own journeys of enlargement.

In the end, the pages of this book are not the conclusion; they are the prologue to a new chapter in your life. Embrace the principles, live them, and watch as your story unfolds with the brilliance of enlargement and prosperity.

Wishing you a life filled with abundance, impact, and continuous growth.

Warm regards,

Joshua Selman

PRINCIPLES FOR ENLARGEMENT

PRINCIPLES FOR ENLARGEMENT

PRINCIPLES FOR ENLARGEMENT

PRINCIPLES FOR ENLARGEMENT